DOVER · THRIFT · EDITIONS

"Lord Randal"
and
Other British Ballads

COLLECTED BY
Francis James Child

DOVER PUBLICATIONS, INC.
New York

DOVER THRIFT EDITIONS

GENERAL EDITOR: STANLEY APPELBAUM

Copyright

Published in Canada by General Publishing Company, Ltd., 30 Lesmill Road, Don Mills, Toronto, Ontario.

Published in the United Kingdom by Constable and Company, Ltd., 3 The Lanchesters, 162–164 Fulham Palace Road, London W6 9ER.

Bibliographical Note

The present edition, first published by Dover Publications, Inc., in 1996, is a new selection of 29 poems reprinted from *English and Scottish Popular Ballads: Cambridge Edition* (edited by Helen Child Sargent and George Lyman Kittredge on the basis of F. J. Child's complete 1882–1898 collection), as published by Houghton, Mifflin and Company, Boston (The Riverside Press, Cambridge), in 1904. See the new Note, specially prepared for the present volume, for further bibliographical data. Other new features of this volume are a Glossary and Alphabetical Lists of Titles and First Lines.

Library of Congress Cataloging-in-Publication Data

Child, Francis James, 1825–1896.
    Lord Randal and other British ballads / collected by Francis James Child.
        p.   cm. — (Dover thrift editions)
    "A new selection of 29 poems reprinted from English and Scottish popular ballads . . . as published by Houghton, Mifflin and Company, Boston . . . in 1904"—T.p. verso.
    Includes index.
    ISBN 0-486-28987-7 (pbk.)
    1. Ballads, English—Great Britain—Texts. 2. Narrative poetry, English. 3. Great Britain—Poetry. I. Title. II. Series.
PR1181.C5   1996
821'.04408—dc20
                                        95-38267
                                            CIP

Manufactured in the United States of America
Dover Publications, Inc., 31 East 2nd Street, Mineola, N.Y. 11501

Note

Ballads are short (or relatively short) narrative poems. Anonymous ballads are a rich part of the literary heritage of many nations, and many ballad themes have crossed national lines. The English-language tradition is particularly abundant and influential. Ballads, either recited or sung, are part of our everyday mentality. They have been cited in great works of literature (as in Coleridge's poem "Dejection: An Ode," which refers to the ballad "Sir Patrick Spens") and have been imitated by well-known poets (as in Keats's "La Belle Dame sans Merci"). They have immigrated from Britain to the United States, where such regions as the Appalachians have preserved the living tradition.

If the English-language anonymous ballads are so well known and meaningful to us today, it is largely thanks to the collecting efforts of Francis James Child (born in Boston 1825, died there 1896); in fact, they are often referred to as "Child ballads" because of him. Child published eight volumes of ballads in 1857 and 1858, but the definitive edition was not to be published until much later: in ten parts (later assembled into five volumes) published by Houghton, Mifflin and Company, Boston, between 1882 and 1898. In 1904 the same publisher issued a handy volume of selections from the magnum opus, skillfully edited by the great Bostonian scholar George Lyman Kittredge (1860–1941) in association with Helen Child Sargent; the present selection was made from that volume.

The definitive Child collection (the framework of which was retained by Sargent and Kittredge) contains 305 different ballads, many of which are represented by a number of versions, the various versions under each ballad number being indicated by sequential letters (A, B, C, etc.). The table of contents of the present volume supplies the Child number and letter for every item chosen. The present selection, while necessarily avoiding the longest poems no matter how famous (thus, for instance, "Chevy Chase" and the long ballads of the Robin Hood cycle could not be included), attempts to represent most of the ballad genres with outstanding examples, famous and influential; of the various versions of a given ballad, the most interesting and/or the most complete has been chosen in each case.

The ballad of the uncanny, in which human beings come into dangerous contact with the supernatural, is represented by such poems as "Lady Isabel and the Elf-Knight" and "Thomas Rymer" (associated with the Tannhäuser legend); the ballads of stark family tragedy, by "The Twa Sisters," "Edward" and a number of others. Human beings changed into, or married to, animals are to be found in "The Laily Worm and the Machrel of the Sea" and "The Great Silkie of Sule Skerry." Romance, whether happy or otherwise, is represented by "Fair Margaret and Sweet William," "Bonny Barbara Allan" and others; Scottish history and border conflicts by "Mary Hamilton," "Johnie Armstrong" and more; and humor by "Get Up and Bar the Door" and "The Farmer's Curst Wife."

Each version included here is complete, and in the exact form and spelling of Child's text. The titles are exactly in his wording, as well, even when it conflicts with the spelling in the particular ballad version selected here (thus, the title "Bonny Barbara Allan" clashes with the spelling "Allen" in the text). The glossary in the present volume, giving the meaning of terms in Scottish dialect and identifying more usual English words that may be disguised by an older odd spelling, has been adapted to fit our selection from the glossary in the 1904 volume.

Contents

The numbers in parentheses refer to the location of these ballads in Child's complete collection; the letters refer to the specific versions included here.

v

Lady Isabel and the Elf-Knight

1 Fair lady Isabel sits in her bower sewing,
    Aye as the gowans grow gay.
There she heard an elf-knight blawing his horn,
    The first morning in May.

2 'If I had yon horn that I hear blawing,
And yon elf-knight to sleep in my bosom.'

3 This maiden had scarcely these words spoken,
Till in at her window the elf-knight has luppen.

4 'It 's a very strange matter, fair maiden,' said he,
'I canna blaw my horn but ye call on me.

5 'But will ye go to yon greenwood side?
If ye canna gang, I will cause you to ride.'

6 He leapt on a horse, and she on another,
And they rode on to the greenwood together.

7 'Light down, light down, lady Isabel,' said he,
'We are come to the place where ye are to die.'

8 'Hae mercy, hae mercy, kind sir, on me,
Till ance my dear father and mother I see.'

9 'Seven king's-daughters here hae I slain,
And ye shall be the eight o them.'

10 'O sit down a while, lay your head on my knee,
That we may hae some rest before that I die.'

11 She stroak'd him sae fast, the nearer he did creep,
Wi a sma charm she lulld him fast asleep.

12 Wi his ain sword-belt sae fast as she ban him,
Wi his ain dag-durk sae sair as she dang him.

13 'If seven king's-daughters here ye hae slain,
Lye ye here, a husband to them a'.'

1

The Twa Sisters

1 There was twa sisters in a bowr,
      (Edinburgh, Edinburgh)
   There was twa sisters in a bowr,
      (Stirling for ay)
   There was twa sisters in a bowr,
   There came a knight to be their wooer.
      Bonny Saint Johnston stands upon Tay.

2 He courted the eldest wi glove an ring,
   But he lovd the youngest above a' thing.

3 He courted the eldest wi brotch an knife,
   But lovd the youngest as his life.

4 The eldest she was vexed sair,
   An much envi'd her sister fair.

5 Into her bowr she could not rest,
   Wi grief an spite she almos brast.

6 Upon a morning fair an clear,
   She cried upon her sister dear:

7 'O sister, come to yon sea stran,
   An see our father's ships come to lan.'

8 She 's taen her by the milk-white han,
   An led her down to yon sea stran.

9 The youngest stood upon a stane,
   The eldest came an threw her in.

10 She tooke her by the middle sma,
    An dashd her bonny back to the jaw.

11 'O sister, sister, tak my han,
    An Ise mack you heir to a' my lan.

12 'O sister, sister, tak my middle,
    An yes get my goud and my gouden girdle.

13 'O sister, sister, save my life,
    An I swear Ise never be nae man's wife.'

14 'Foul fa the han that I should tacke,
   It twin'd me an my wardles make.

15 'Your cherry cheeks an yellow hair
   Gars me gae maiden for evermair.'

16 Sometimes she sank, an sometimes she swam,
   Till she came down yon bonny mill-dam.

17 O out it came the miller's son,
   An saw the fair maid swimmin in.

18 'O father, father, draw your dam,
   Here 's either a mermaid or a swan.'

19 The miller quickly drew the dam,
   An there he found a drownd woman.

20 You coudna see her yellow hair
   For gold and pearle that were so rare.

21 You coudna see her middle sma
   For gouden girdle that was sae braw.

22 You coudna see her fingers white,
   For gouden rings that was sae gryte.

23 An by there came a harper fine,
   That harped to the king at dine.

24 When he did look that lady upon,
   He sighd and made a heavy moan.

25 He 's taen three locks o her yellow hair,
   An wi them strung his harp sae fair.

26 The first tune he did play and sing,
   Was, 'Farewell to my father the king.'

27 The nextin tune that he playd syne,
   Was, 'Farewell to my mother the queen.'

28 The lasten tune that he playd then,
   Was, 'Wae to my sister, fair Ellen.'

The Cruel Brother

1 There was three ladies playd at the ba,
       With a hey ho and a lillie gay
   There came a knight and played oer them a'.
       As the primrose spreads so sweetly.

2 The eldest was baith tall and fair,
   But the youngest was beyond compare.

3 The midmost had a graceful mien,
   But the youngest lookd like beautie's queen.

4 The knight bowd low to a' the three,
   But to the youngest he bent his knee.

5 The ladie turned her head aside,
   The knight he woo'd her to be his bride.

6 The ladie blushd a rosy red,
   And sayd, 'Sir knight, I 'm too young to wed.'

7 'O ladie fair, give me your hand,
   And I 'll make you ladie of a' my land.'

8 'Sir knight, ere ye my favor win,
   You maun get consent frae a' my kin.'

9 He 's got consent frae her parents dear,
   And likewise frae her sisters fair.

10 He 's got consent frae her kin each one,
    But forgot to spiek to her brother John.

11 Now, when the wedding day was come,
    The knight would take his bonny bride home.

12 And many a lord and many a knight
    Came to behold that ladie bright.

13 And there was nae man that did her see,
    But wishd himself bridegroom to be.

14 Her father dear led her down the stair,
    And her sisters twain they kissd her there.

15 Her mother dear led her thro the closs,
And her brother John set her on her horse.

16 She leand her oer the saddle-bow,
To give him a kiss ere she did go.

17 He has taen a knife, baith lang and sharp,
And stabbd that bonny bride to the heart.

18 She hadno ridden half thro the town,
Until her heart's blude staind her gown.

19 'Ride softly on,' says the best young man,
'For I think our bonny bride looks pale and wan.'

20 'O lead me gently up yon hill,
And I 'll there sit down, and make my will.'

21 'O what will you leave to your father dear?'
'The silver-shode steed that brought me here.'

22 'What will you leave to your mother dear?'
'My velvet pall and my silken gear.'

23 'What will you leave to your sister Anne?'
'My silken scarf and my gowden fan.'

24 'What will you leave to your sister Grace?'
'My bloody cloaths to wash and dress.'

25 'What will you leave to your brother John?'
'The gallows-tree to hang him on.'

26 'What will you leave to your brother John's wife?'
'The wilderness to end her life.'

27 This ladie fair in her grave was laid,
And many a mass was oer her said.

28 But it would have made your heart right sair,
To see the bridegroom rive his haire.

Lord Randal

1 'O where ha you been, Lord Randal, my son?
And where ha you been, my handsome young man?'
'I ha been at the greenwood; mother, mak my bed soon,
For I 'm wearied wi hunting, and fain wad lie down.'

2 'An wha met ye there, Lord Randal, my son?
   An wha met you there, my handsome young man?'
   'O I met wi my true-love; mother, mak my bed soon,
   For I 'm wearied wi huntin, an fain wad lie down.'

3 'And what did she give you, Lord Randal, my son?
   And what did she give you, my handsome young man?'
   'Eels fried in a pan; mother, mak my bed soon,
   For I 'm wearied wi huntin, and fain wad lie down.'

4 'And wha gat your leavins, Lord Randal, my son?
   And wha gat your leavins, my handsom young man?'
   'My hawks and my hounds; mother, mak my bed soon,
   For I 'm wearied wi hunting, and fain wad lie down.'

5 'And what becam of them, Lord Randal, my son?
   And what becam of them, my handsome young man?'
   'They stretched their legs out an died; mother, mak my bed soon,
   For I 'm wearied wi huntin, and fain wad lie down.'

6 'O I fear you are poisoned, Lord Randal, my son!
   I fear you are poisoned, my handsome young man!'
   'O yes, I am poisoned; mother, mak my bed soon,
   For I 'm sick at the heart, and I fain wad lie down.'

7 'What d' ye leave to your mother, Lord Randal, my son?
   What d' ye leave to your mother, my handsome young man?'
   'Four and twenty milk kye; mother, mak my bed soon,
   For I 'm sick at the heart, and I fain wad lie down.'

8 'What d' ye leave to your sister, Lord Randal, my son?
   What d' ye leave to your sister, my handsome young man?'
   'My gold and my silver; mother, mak my bed soon,
   For I 'm sick at the heart, an I fain wad lie down.'

9 'What d' ye leave to your brother, Lord Randal, my son?
   What d' ye leave to your brother, my handsome young man?'
   'My houses and my lands; mother, mak my bed soon,
   For I 'm sick at the heart, and I fain wad lie down.'

10 'What d' ye leave to your true-love, Lord Randal, my son?
    What d' ye leave to your true-love, my handsome young man?'
    'I leave her hell and fire; mother, mak my bed soon,
    For I 'm sick at the heart, and I fain wad lie down.'

Edward

1 'Why dois your brand sae drap wi bluid,
                    Edward, Edward,
Why dois your brand sae drap wi bluid,
    And why sae sad gang yee O?'
'O I hae killed my hauke sae guid,
                    Mither, mither,
O I hae killed my hauke sae guid,
    And I had nae mair bot hee O.'

2 'Your haukis bluid was nevir sae reid,
                    Edward, Edward,
Your haukis bluid was nevir sae reid,
    My deir son I tell thee O.'
'O I hae killed my reid-roan steid,
                    Mither, mither,
O I hae killed my reid-roan steid,
    That erst was sae fair and frie O.'

3 'Your steid was auld, and ye hae gat mair,
                    Edward, Edward,
Your steid was auld, and ye hae gat mair,
    Sum other dule ye drie O.'
'O I hae killed my fadir deir,
                    Mither, mither,
O I hae killed my fadir deir,
    Alas, and wae is mee O!'

4 'And whatten penance wul ye drie for that,
                    Edward, Edward?
And whatten penance will ye drie for that?
    My deir son, now tell me O.'
'Ile set my feit in yonder boat,
                    Mither, mither,
Ile set my feit in yonder boat,
    And Ile fare ovir the sea O.'

5 'And what wul ye doe wi your towirs and your ha,
                    Edward, Edward?
And what wul ye doe wi your towirs and your ha,
    That were sae fair to see O?'

'Ile let thame stand tul they doun fa,
        Mither, mither,
Ile let thame stand tul they doun fa,
    For here nevir mair maun I bee O.'

6 'And what wul ye leive to your bairns and your wife,
        Edward, Edward?
And what wul ye leive to your bairns and your wife,
    Whan ye gang ovir the sea O?'
'The warldis room, late them beg thrae life,
        Mither, mither,
The warldis room, late them beg thrae life,
    For thame nevir mair wul I see O.'

7 'And what wul ye leive to your ain mither deir,
        Edward, Edward?
And what wul ye leive to your ain mither deir?
    My deir son, now tell me O.'
'The curse of hell frae me sall ye beir,
        Mither, mither,
The curse of hell frae me sall ye beir,
    Sic counseils ye gave to me O.'

The Three Ravens

1 There were three rauens sat on a tree,
        Downe a downe, hay down, hay downe
There were three rauens sat on a tree,
    With a downe
There were three rauens sat on a tree,
They were as blacke as they might be.
        With a downe derrie, derrie, derrie, downe, downe

2 The one of them said to his mate,
    'Where shall we our breakefast take?'

3 'Downe in yonder greene field,
    There lies a knight slain vnder his shield.

4 'His hounds they lie downe at his feete,
    So well they can their master keepe.

5 'His haukes they flie so eagerly,
    There 's no fowle dare him come nie.'

6 Downe there comes a fallow doe,
   As great with yong as she might goe.

7 She lift vp his bloudy hed,
   And kist his wounds that were so red.

8 She got him vp vpon her backe,
   And carried him to earthen lake.

9 She buried him before the prime,
   She was dead herselfe ere euen-song time.

10 God send euery gentleman,
   Such haukes, such hounds, and such a leman.

Kemp Owyne

1 Her mother died when she was young,
      Which gave her cause to make great moan;
   Her father married the warst woman
      That ever lived in Christendom.

2 She served her with foot and hand,
      In every thing that she could dee,
   Till once, in an unlucky time,
      She threw her in ower Craigy's sea.

3 Says, 'Lie you there, dove Isabel,
      And all my sorrows lie with thee;
   Till Kemp Owyne come ower the sea,
      And borrow you with kisses three,
   Let all the warld do what they will,
      Oh borrowed shall you never be!'

4 Her breath grew strang, her hair grew lang,
      And twisted thrice about the tree,
   And all the people, far and near,
      Thought that a savage beast was she.

5 These news did come to Kemp Owyne,
      Where he lived, far beyond the sea;
   He hasted him to Craigy's sea,
      And on the savage beast lookd he.

6 Her breath was strang, her hair was lang,
    And twisted was about the tree,
  And with a swing she came about:
    'Come to Craigy's sea, and kiss with me.

7 'Here is a royal belt,' she cried,
    'That I have found in the green sea;
  And while your body it is on,
    Drawn shall your blood never be;
  But if you touch me, tail or fin,
    I vow my belt your death shall be.'

8 He stepped in, gave her a kiss,
    The royal belt he brought him wi;
  Her breath was strang, her hair was lang,
    And twisted twice about the tree,
  And with a swing she came about:
    'Come to Craigy's sea, and kiss with me.

9 'Here is a royal ring,' she said,
    'That I have found in the green sea;
  And while your finger it is on,
    Drawn shall your blood never be;
  But if you touch me, tail or fin,
    I swear my ring your death shall be.'

10 He stepped in, gave her a kiss,
    The royal ring he brought him wi;
  Her breath was strang, her hair was lang,
    And twisted ance about the tree,
  And with a swing she came about:
    'Come to Craigy's sea, and kiss with me.

11 'Here is a royal brand,' she said,
    'That I have found in the green sea;
  And while your body it is on,
    Drawn shall your blood never be;
  But if you touch me, tail or fin,
    I swear my brand your death shall be.'

12 He stepped in, gave her a kiss,
    The royal brand he brought him wi;
  Her breath was sweet, her hair grew short,
    And twisted nane about the tree,
  And smilingly she came about,
    As fair a woman as fair could be.

The Laily Worm and the Machrel of the Sea

1 'I was bat seven year alld
    Fan my mider she did dee,
My father marrëd the ae warst woman
    The wardle did ever see.

2 'For she has made me the lailly worm
    That lays att the fitt of the tree,
An o my sister Meassry
    The machrel of the sea.

3 'An every Saterday att noon
    The machrl comes to me,
An she takes my laylë head,
    An lays it on her knee,
An keames it we a silver kemm,
    An washes it in the sea.

4 'Seven knights ha I slain
    Sane I lay att the fitt of the tree;
An ye war na my ain father,
    The eight an ye sud be.'

5 'Sing on your song, ye laily worm,
    That ye sung to me;'
'I never sung that song
    But fatt I wad sing to ye.

6 'I was but seven year aull
    Fan my mider she did dee,
My father marrëd the a warst woman
    The wardle did ever see.

7 'She changed me to the layely worm
    That layes att the fitt of the tree,
An my sister Messry
    To the makrell of the sea.

8 'And every Saterday att noon
    The machrell comes to me,
An she takes my layly head,
    An layes it on her knee,
An kames it weth a siller kame,
    An washes it in the sea.

9 'Seven knights ha I slain
    San I lay att the fitt of the tree;
An ye war na my ain father,
    The eight ye sud be.'

10 He sent for his lady
    As fast as sen cod he:
'Far is my son,
    That ye sent fra me,
And my daughter,
    Lady Messry?'

11 'Yer son is att our king's court,
    Sarving for meatt an fee,
And yer daughter is att our quin's court,
    A mary suit an free.'

12 'Ye lee, ye ill woman,
    Sa loud as I hear ye lea,
For my son is the layelly worm
    That lays at the fitt of the tree,
An my daughter Messry
    The machrell of the sea.'

13 She has tain a silver wan
    An gine him stroks three,
An he started up the bravest knight
    Your eyes did ever see.

14 She has tane a small horn
    An loud an shill blue she,
An a' the fish came her tell but the proud machrell,
    An she stood by the sea:
Ye shaped me ance an unshemly shape,
    An ye 's never mare shape me.'

15 He has sent to the wood
    For hathorn an fun,
An he has tane that gay lady,
    An ther he did her burne.

Thomas Rymer

1 True Thomas lay oer yond grassy bank,
    And he beheld a ladie gay,
A ladie that was brisk and bold,
    Come riding oer the fernie brae.

2 Her skirt was of the grass-green silk,
    Her mantel of the velvet fine,
At ilka tett of her horse's mane
    Hung fifty silver bells and nine.

3 True Thomas he took off his hat,
    And bowed him low down till his knee:
'All hail, thou mighty Queen of Heaven!
    For your peer on earth I never did see.'

4 'O no, O no, True Thomas,' she says,
    'That name does not belong to me;
I am but the queen of fair Elfland,
    And I 'm come here for to visit thee.

     *   *   *   *   *

5 'But ye maun go wi me now, Thomas,
    True Thomas, ye maun go wi me,
For ye maun serve me seven years,
    Thro weel or wae as may chance to be.'

6 She turned about her milk-white steed,
    And took True Thomas up behind,
And aye wheneer her bridle rang,
    The steed flew swifter than the wind.

7 For forty days and forty nights
    He wade thro red blude to the knee,
And he saw neither sun nor moon,
    But heard the roaring of the sea.

8 O they rade on, and further on,
    Until they came to a garden green:
'Light down, light down, ye ladie free,
    Some of that fruit let me pull to thee.'

9 'O no, O no, True Thomas,' she says,
    'That fruit maun not be touched by thee,
For a' the plagues that are in hell
    Light on the fruit of this countrie.

10 'But I have a loaf here in my lap,
    Likewise a bottle of claret wine,
And now ere we go farther on,
    We 'll rest a while, and ye may dine.'

11 When he had eaten and drunk his fill,
    'Lay down your head upon my knee,'
The lady sayd, 'ere we climb yon hill,
    And I will show you fairlies three.

12 'O see not ye yon narrow road,
    So thick beset wi thorns and briers?
That is the path of righteousness,
    Tho after it but few enquires.

13 'And see not ye that braid braid road,
    That lies across yon lillie leven?
That is the path of wickedness,
    Tho some call it the road to heaven.

14 'And see not ye that bonny road,
    Which winds about the fernie brae?
That is the road to fair Elfland,
    Where you and I this night maun gae.

15 'But Thomas, ye maun hold your tongue,
    Whatever you may hear or see,
For gin ae word you should chance to speak,
    You will neer get back to your ain countrie.'

16 He has gotten a coat of the even cloth,
    And a pair of shoes of velvet green,
And till seven years were past and gone
    True Thomas on earth was never seen.

The Wee Wee Man

1 As I was wa'king all alone,
    Between a water and a wa,
And there I spy'd a wee wee man,
    And he was the least that ere I saw.

2 His legs were scarce a shathmont's length,
  And thick and thimber was his thigh;
Between his brows there was a span,
  And between his shoulders there was three.

3 He took up a meikle stane,
  And he flang 't as far as I could see;
Though I had been a Wallace wight,
  I couldna liften 't to my knee.

4 'O wee wee man, but thou be strang!
  O tell me where thy dwelling be?'
'My dwelling 's down at yon bonny bower;
  O will you go with me and see?'

5 On we lap, and awa we rade,
  Till we came to yon bonny green;
We lighted down for to bait our horse,
  And out there came a lady fine.

6 Four and twenty at her back,
  And they were a' clad out in green;
Though the King of Scotland had been there,
  The warst o them might hae been his queen.

7 On we lap, and awa we rade,
  Till we came to yon bonny ha,
Whare the roof was o the beaten gould,
  And the floor was o the cristal a'.

8 When we came to the stair-foot,
  Ladies were dancing, jimp and sma,
But in the twinkling of an eye,
  My wee wee man was clean awa.

The Twa Brothers

1 There were twa brethren in the north,
  They went to school thegithar;
The one unto the other said,
  Will you try a warsle afore?

2 They wrestled up, they wrestled down,
  Till Sir John fell to the ground,

And there was a knife in Sir Willie's pouch,
  Gied him a deadlie wound.

3 'Oh brither dear, take me on your back,
   Carry me to yon burn clear,
 And wash the blood from off my wound,
   And it will bleed nae mair.'

4 He took him up upon his back,
   Carried him to yon burn clear,
 And washd the blood from off his wound,
   And aye it bled the mair.

5 'Oh brother dear, take me on your back,
   Carry me to yon kirk-yard,
 And dig a grave baith wide and deep,
   And lay my body there.'

6 He 's taen him up upon his back,
   Carried him to yon kirk-yard,
 And dug a grave both deep and wide,
   And laid his body there.

7 'But what will I say to my father dear,
   Should he chance to say, Willie, whar 's John?'
 'Oh say that he 's to England gone,
   To buy him a cask of wine.'

8 'And what shall I say to my mother dear,
   Should she chance to say, Willie, whar 's John?'
 'Oh say that he 's to England gone,
   To buy her a new silk gown.'

9 'And what will I say to my sister dear,
   Should she chance to say, Willie, whar 's John?'
 'Oh say that he 's to England gone,
   To buy her a wedding ring.'

10 'What will I say to her you loe dear,
    Should she cry, Why tarries my John?'
  'Oh tell her I lie in fair Kirk-land,
    And home will never come.'

Sir Patrick Spens

1 The king sits in Dumferling toune,
    Drinking the blude-reid wine:
  'O whar will I get guid sailor,
    To sail this schip of mine?'

2 Up and spak an eldern knicht,
    Sat at the kings richt kne:
  'Sir Patrick Spence is the best sailor
    That sails upon the se.'

3 The king has written a braid letter,
    And signd it wi his hand,
  And sent it to Sir Patrick Spence,
    Was walking on the sand.

4 The first line that Sir Patrick red,
    A loud lauch lauched he;
  The next line that Sir Patrick red,
    The teir blinded his ee.

5 'O wha is this has don this deid,
    This ill deid don to me,
  To send me out this time o' the yeir,
    To sail upon the se!

6 'Mak hast, mak haste, my mirry men all,
    Our guid schip sails the morne:'
  'O say na sae, my master deir,
    For I feir a deadlie storme.

7 'Late late yestreen I saw the new moone,
    Wi the auld moone in hir arme,
  And I feir, I feir, my deir master,
    That we will cum to harme.'

8 O our Scots nobles wer richt laith
    To weet their cork-heild schoone;
  Bot lang owre a' the play wer playd,
    Thair hats they swam aboone.

9 O lang, lang may their ladies sit,
    Wi thair fans into their hand,

Or eir they se Sir Patrick Spence
    Cum sailing to the land.

10 O lang, lang may the ladies stand,
    Wi thair gold kems in their hair,
  Waiting for thair ain deir lords,
    For they 'll se thame na mair.

11 Haf owre, haf owre to Aberdour,
    It 's fiftie fadom deip,
  And thair lies guid Sir Patrick Spence,
    Wi the Scots lords at his feit.

Fair Annie

1 'It 's narrow, narrow, make your bed,
    And learn to lie your lane;
  For I 'm ga'n oer the sea, Fair Annie,
    A braw bride to bring hame.
  Wi her I will get gowd and gear;
    Wi you I neer got nane.

2 'But wha will bake my bridal bread,
    Or brew my bridal ale?
  And wha will welcome my brisk bride,
    That I bring oer the dale?'

3 'It 's I will bake your bridal bread,
    And brew your bridal ale,
  And I will welcome your brisk bride,
    That you bring oer the dale.'

4 'But she that welcomes my brisk bride
    Maun gang like maiden fair;
  She maun lace on her robe sae jimp,
    And braid her yellow hair.'

5 'But how can I gang maiden-like,
    When maiden I am nane?
  Have I not born seven sons to thee,
    And am with child again?'

6 She 's taen her young son in her arms,
    Another in her hand,
And she 's up to the highest tower,
    To see him come to land.

7 'Come up, come up, my eldest son,
    And look oer yon sea-strand,
And see your father's new-come bride,
    Before she come to land.'

8 'Come down, come down, my mother dear,
    Come frae the castle wa!
I fear, if langer ye stand there,
    Ye 'll let yoursell down fa.'

9 And she gaed down, and farther down,
    Her love's ship for to see,
And the topmast and the mainmast
    Shone like the silver free.

10 And she 's gane down, and farther down,
    The bride's ship to behold,
And the topmast and the mainmast
    They shone just like the gold.

11 She 's taen her seven sons in her hand,
    I wot she didna fail;
She met Lord Thomas and his bride,
    As they came oer the dale.

12 'You 're welcome to your house, Lord Thomas,
    You 're welcome to your land;
You 're welcome with your fair ladye,
    That you lead by the hand.

13 'You 're welcome to your ha's, ladye,
    You 're welcome to your bowers;
You 're welcome to your hame, ladye,
    For a' that 's here is yours.'

14 'I thank thee, Annie; I thank thee, Annie,
    Sae dearly as I thank thee;
You 're the likest to my sister Annie,
    That ever I did see.

15 'There came a knight out oer the sea,
    And steald my sister away;
  The shame scoup in his company,
    And land whereer he gae!'

16 She hang ae napkin at the door,
    Another in the ha,
  And a' to wipe the trickling tears,
    Sae fast as they did fa.

17 And aye she served the lang tables,
    With white bread and with wine,
  And aye she drank the wan water,
    To had her colour fine.

18 And aye she served the lang tables,
    With white bread and with brown;
  And ay she turned her round about,
    Sae fast the tears fall down.

19 And he 's taen down the silk napkin,
    Hung on a silver pin,
  And aye he wipes the tear trickling
    A' down her cheik and chin.

20 And aye he turn'd him round about,
    And smil'd amang his men;
  Says, Like ye best the old ladye,
    Or her that 's new come hame?

21 When bells were rung, and mass was sung,
    And a' men bound to bed,
  Lord Thomas and his new-come bride
    To their chamber they were gaed.

22 Annie made her bed a little forbye,
    To hear what they might say;
  'And ever alas!' Fair Annie cried,
    'That I should see this day!

23 'Gin my seven sons were seven young rats,
    Running on the castle wa,
  And I were a grey cat mysell,
    I soon would worry them a'.

24 'Gin my seven sons were seven young hares,
        Running oer yon lilly lee,
    And I were a grew hound mysell,
        Soon worried they a' should be.'

25 And wae and sad Fair Annie sat,
        And drearie was her sang,
    And ever, as she sobbd and grat,
        'Wae to the man that did the wrang!'

26 'My gown is on,' said the new-come bride,
        'My shoes are on my feet,
    And I will to Fair Annie's chamber,
        And see what gars her greet.

27 'What ails ye, what ails ye, Fair Annie,
        That ye make sic a moan?
    Has your wine barrels cast the girds,
        Or is your white bread gone?

28 'O wha was 't was your father, Annie,
        Or wha was 't was your mother?
    And had ye ony sister, Annie,
        Or had ye ony brother?'

29 'The Earl of Wemyss was my father,
        The Countess of Wemyss my mother;
    And a' the folk about the house
        To me were sister and brother.'

30 'If the Earl of Wemyss was your father,
        I wot sae was he mine;
    And it shall not be for lack o gowd
        That ye your love sall tine.

31 'For I have seven ships o mine ain,
        A' loaded to the brim,
    And I will gie them a' to thee,
        Wi four to thine eldest son:
    But thanks to a' the powers in heaven
        That I gae maiden hame!'

Lady Maisry

1 The young lords o the north country
    Have all a wooing gone,
To win the love of Lady Maisry,
    But o them she woud hae none.

2 O they hae courted Lady Maisry
    Wi a' kin kind of things;
An they hae sought her Lady Maisry
    Wi brotches an wi rings.

3 An they ha sought her Lady Maisry
    Frae father and frae mother;
An they ha sought her Lady Maisry
    Frae sister an frae brother.

4 An they ha followd her Lady Maisry
    Thro chamber an thro ha;
But a' that they coud say to her,
    Her answer still was Na.

5 'O had your tongues, young men,' she says,
    'An think nae mair o me;
For I 've gien my love to an English lord,
    An think nae mair o me.'

6 Her father's kitchy-boy heard that,
    An ill death may he dee!
An he is on to her brother,
    As fast as gang coud he.

7 'O is my father an my mother well,
    But an my brothers three?
Gin my sister Lady Maisry be well,
    There 's naething can ail me.'

8 'Your father and your mother is well,
    But an your brothers three;
Your sister Lady Maisry 's well,
    So big wi bairn gangs she.'

9 'Gin this be true you tell to me,
    My mailison light on thee!

But gin it be a lie you tell,
    You sal be hangit hie.'

10 He 's done him to his sister's bowr,
    Wi meikle doole an care;
An there he saw her Lady Maisry,
    Kembing her yallow hair.

11 'O wha is aught that bairn,' he says,
    'That ye sae big are wi?
And gin ye winna own the truth,
    This moment ye sall dee.'

12 She turnd her right an roun about,
    An the kem fell frae her han;
A trembling seizd her fair body,
    An her rosy cheek grew wan.

13 'O pardon me, my brother dear,
    An the truth I 'll tell to thee;
My bairn it is to Lord William,
    An he is betrothd to me.'

14 'O coud na ye gotten dukes, or lords,
    Intill your ain country,
That ye draw up wi an English dog,
    To bring this shame on me?

15 'But ye maun gi up the English lord,
    Whan youre young babe is born;
For, gin you keep by him an hour langer,
    Your life sall be forlorn.'

16 'I will gi up this English blood,
    Till my young babe be born;
But the never a day nor hour langer,
    Tho my life should be forlorn.'

17 'O whare is a' my merry young men,
    Whom I gi meat and fee,
To pu the thistle and the thorn,
    To burn this wile whore wi?'

18 'O whare will I get a bonny boy,
    To help me in my need,
To rin wi hast to Lord William,
    And bid him come wi speed?'

19 O out it spake a bonny boy,
      Stood by her brother's side:
    'O I would rin your errand, lady,
      Oer a' the world wide.

20 'Aft have I run your errands, lady,
      Whan blawn baith win and weet;
    But now I 'll rin your errand, lady,
      Wi sat tears on my cheek.'

21 O whan he came to broken briggs,
      He bent his bow and swam,
    An whan he came to the green grass growin,
      He slackd his shoone and ran.

22 O whan he came to Lord William's gates,
      He baed na to chap or ca,
    But set his bent bow till his breast,
      An lightly lap the wa;
    An, or the porter was at the gate,
      The boy was i the ha.

23 'O is my biggins broken, boy?
      Or is my towers won?
    Or is my lady lighter yet,
      Of a dear daughter or son?'

24 'Your biggin is na broken, sir,
      Nor is your towers won;
    But the fairest lady in a' the lan
      For you this day maun burn.'

25 'O saddle me the black, the black,
      Or saddle me the brown;
    O saddle me the swiftest steed
      That ever rade frae a town.'

26 Or he was near a mile awa,
      She heard his wild horse sneeze:
    'Mend up the fire, my false brother,
      It 's na come to my knees.'

27 O whan he lighted at the gate,
      She heard his bridle ring:
    'Mend up the fire, my false brother,
      It 's far yet frae my chin.

28 'Mend up the fire to me, brother,
    Mend up the fire to me;
  For I see him comin hard an fast
    Will soon men 't up to thee.

29 'O gin my hands had been loose, Willy,
    Sae hard as they are boun,
  I would have turnd me frae the gleed,
    And castin out your young son.'

30 'O I 'll gar burn for you, Maisry,
    Your father an your mother;
  An I 'll gar burn for you, Maisry,
    Your sister an your brother.

31 'An I 'll gar burn for you, Maisry,
    The chief of a' your kin;
  An the last bonfire that I come to,
    Mysel I will cast in.'

Fair Margaret and Sweet William

1 As it fell out on a long summer's day,
    Two lovers they sat on a hill;
  They sat together that long summer's day,
    And could not talk their fill.

2 'I see no harm by you, Margaret,
    Nor you see none by me;
  Before tomorrow eight a clock
    A rich wedding shall you see.'

3 Fair Margaret sat in her bower-window,
    A combing of her hair,
  And there she spy'd Sweet William and his bride,
    As they were riding near.

4 Down she layd her ivory comb,
    And up she bound her hair;
  She went her way forth of her bower,
    But never more did come there.

5 When day was gone, and night was come,
      And all men fast asleep,
   Then came the spirit of Fair Margaret,
      And stood at William's feet.

6 'God give you joy, you two true lovers,
      In bride-bed fast asleep;
   Loe I am going to my green grass grave,
      And am in my winding-sheet.'

7 When day was come, and night was gone,
      And all men wak'd from sleep,
   Sweet William to his lady said,
      'My dear, I have cause to weep.

8 'I dreamd a dream, my dear lady;
      Such dreams are never good;
   I dreamd my bower was full of red swine,
      And my bride-bed full of blood.'

9 'Such dreams, such dreams, my honoured lord,
      They never do prove good,
   To dream thy bower was full of swine,
      And thy bride-bed full of blood.'

10 He called up his merry men all,
      By one, by two, and by three,
    Saying, I 'll away to Fair Margaret's bower,
      By the leave of my lady.

11 And when he came to Fair Margaret's bower,
      He knocked at the ring;
    So ready was her seven brethren
      To let Sweet William in.

12 He turned up the covering-sheet:
      'Pray let me see the dead;
    Methinks she does look pale and wan,
      She has lost her cherry red.

13 'I 'll do more for thee, Margaret,
      Than any of thy kin;
    For I will kiss thy pale wan lips,
      Tho a smile I cannot win.'

14 With that bespeak her seven brethren,
       Making most pitious moan:
    'You may go kiss your jolly brown bride,
       And let our sister alone.'

15 'If I do kiss my jolly brown bride,
       I do but what is right;
    For I made no vow to your sister dear,
       By day or yet by night.

16 'Pray tell me then how much you 'll deal
       Of your white bread and your wine;
    So much as is dealt at her funeral today
       Tomorrow shall be dealt at mine.'

17 Fair Margaret dy'd today, today,
       Sweet William he dy'd the morrow;
    Fair Margaret dy'd for pure true love,
       Sweet William he dy'd for sorrow.

18 Margaret was buried in the lower chancel,
       Sweet William in the higher;
    Out of her breast there sprung a rose,
       And out of his a brier.

19 They grew as high as the church-top,
       Till they could grow no higher,
    And then they grew in a true lover's knot,
       Which made all people admire.

20 There came the clerk of the parish,
       As you this truth shall hear,
    And by misfortune cut them down,
       Or they had now been there.

The Unquiet Grave

1 'The wind doth blow today, my love,
       And a few small drops of rain;
    I never had but one true-love,
       In cold grave she was lain.

2 'I 'll do as much for my true-love
    As any young man may;
  I 'll sit and mourn all at her grave
    For a twelvemonth and a day.'

3 The twelvemonth and a day being up,
    The dead began to speak:
  'Oh who sits weeping on my grave,
    And will not let me sleep?'

4 ''T is I, my love, sits on your grave,
    And will not let you sleep;
  For I crave one kiss of your clay-cold lips,
    And that is all I seek.'

5 'You crave one kiss of my clay-cold lips;
    But my breath smells earthy strong;
  If you have one kiss of my clay-cold lips,
    Your time will not be long.

6 ''T is down in yonder garden green,
    Love, where we used to walk,
  The finest flower that ere was seen
    Is withered to a stalk.

7 'The stalk is withered dry, my love,
    So will our hearts decay;
  So make yourself content, my love,
    Till God calls you away.'

The Wife of Usher's Well

1 There lived a wife at Usher's Well,
    And a wealthy wife was she;
  She had three stout and stalwart sons,
    And sent them oer the sea.

2 They hadna been a week from her,
    A week but barely ane,
  Whan word came to the carline wife
    That her three sons were gane.

3 They hadna been a week from her,
     A week but barely three,
  Whan word came to the carlin wife
     That her sons she 'd never see.

4 'I wish the wind may never cease,
     Nor fashes in the flood,
  Till my three sons come hame to me,
     In earthly flesh and blood.'

5 It fell about the Martinmass,
     When nights are lang and mirk,
  The carlin wife's three sons came hame,
     And their hats were o the birk.

6 It neither grew in syke nor ditch,
     Nor yet in ony sheugh;
  But at the gates o Paradise,
     That birk grew fair eneugh.

*   *   *   *   *

7 'Blow up the fire, my maidens,
     Bring water from the well;
  For a' my house shall feast this night,
     Since my three sons are well.'

8 And she has made to them a bed,
     She 's made it large and wide,
  And she 's taen her mantle her about,
     Sat down at the bed-side.

*   *   *   *   *

9 Up then crew the red, red cock,
     And up and crew the gray;
  The eldest to the youngest said,
     'T is time we were away.

10 The cock he hadna crawd but once,
     And clappd his wings at a',
   When the youngest to the eldest said,
     Brother, we must awa.

11 'The cock doth craw, the day doth daw,
     The channerin worm doth chide;
   Gin we be mist out o our place,
     A sair pain we maun bide.

12 'Fare ye weel, my mother dear!
     Fareweel to barn and byre!
   And fare ye weel, the bonny lass
     That kindles my mother's fire!'

Little Musgrave and Lady Barnard

1 As it fell one holy-day,
       Hay downe
     As many be in the yeare,
   When young men and maids together did goe,
     Their mattins and masse to heare,

2 Little Musgrave came to the church-dore;
     The preist was at private masse;
   But he had more minde of the faire women
     Then he had of our lady's grace.

3 The one of them was clad in green,
     Another was clad in pall,
   And then came in my lord Bernard's wife,
     The fairest amonst them all.

4 She cast an eye on Little Musgrave,
     As bright as the summer sun;
   And then bethought this Little Musgrave,
     This lady's heart have I woonn.

5 Quoth she, I have loved thee, Little Musgrave,
     Full long and many a day;
   'So have I loved you, fair lady,
     Yet never word durst I say.'

6 'I have a bower at Buckelsfordbery,
     Full daintyly it is deight;
   If thou wilt wend thither, thou Little Musgrave,
     Thou 's lig in mine armes all night.'

7 Quoth he, I thank yee, faire lady,
     This kindnes thou showest to me;
   But whether it be to my weal or woe,
     This night I will lig with thee.

8 With that he heard, a little tynë page,
      By his ladye's coach as he ran:
   'All though I am my ladye's foot-page,
      Yet I am Lord Barnard's man.

9 'My lord Barnard shall knowe of this,
      Whether I sink or swim;'
   And ever where the bridges were broake
      He laid him downe to swimme.

10 'A sleepe or wake, thou Lord Barnard,
       As thou art a man of life,
    For Little Musgrave is at Bucklesfordbery,
       A bed with thy own wedded wife.'

11 'If this be true, thou little tinny page,
       This thing thou tellest to me,
    Then all the land in Bucklesfordbery
       I freely will give to thee.

12 'But if it be a ly, thou little tinny page,
       This thing thou tellest to me,
    On the hyest tree in Bucklesfordbery
       Then hanged shalt thou be.'

13 He called up his merry men all:
       'Come saddle me my steed;
    This night must I to Buckellsfordbery,
       For I never had greater need.'

14 And some of them whistld, and some of them sung,
       And some these words did say,
    And ever when my lord Barnard's horn blew,
       'Away, Musgrave, away!'

15 'Methinks I hear the thresel-cock,
       Methinks I hear the jaye;
    Methinks I hear my lord Barnard,
       And I would I were away.'

16 'Lye still, lye still, thou Little Musgrave,
       And huggell me from the cold;
    'T is nothing but a shephard's boy,
       A driving his sheep to the fold.

17 'Is not thy hawke upon a perch?
        Thy steed eats oats and hay;
    And thou a fair lady in thine armes,
        And wouldst thou bee away?'

18 With that my lord Barnard came to the dore,
        And lit a stone upon;
    He plucked out three silver keys,
        And he opend the dores each one.

19 He lifted up the coverlett,
        He lifted up the sheet:
    'How now, how now, thou Littell Musgrave,
        Doest thou find my lady sweet?'

20 'I find her sweet,' quoth Little Musgrave,
        'The more 't is to my paine;
    I would gladly give three hundred pounds
        That I were on yonder plaine.'

21 'Arise, arise, thou Littell Musgrave,
        And put thy clothës on;
    It shall nere be said in my country
        I have killed a naked man.

22 'I have two swords in one scabberd,
        Full deere they cost my purse;
    And thou shalt have the best of them,
        And I will have the worse.'

23 The first stroke that Little Musgrave stroke,
        He hurt Lord Barnard sore;
    The next stroke that Lord Barnard stroke,
        Little Musgrave nere struck more.

24 With that bespake this faire lady,
        In bed whereas she lay:
    'Although thou 'rt dead, thou Little Musgrave,
        Yet I for thee will pray.

25 'And wish well to thy soule will I,
        So long as I have life;
    So will I not for thee, Barnard,
        Although I am thy wedded wife.'

26 He cut her paps from off her brest;
        Great pitty it was to see

That some drops of this ladie's heart's blood
    Ran trickling downe her knee.

27 'Woe worth you, woe worth, my mery men all,
    You were nere borne for my good;
Why did you not offer to stay my hand,
    When you see me wax so wood?

28 'For I have slaine the bravest sir knight
    That ever rode on steed;
So have I done the fairest lady
    That ever did woman's deed.

29 'A grave, a grave,' Lord Barnard cryd,
    'To put these lovers in;
But lay my lady on the upper hand,
    For she came of the better kin.'

Bonny Barbara Allan

1 In Scarlet Town, where I was bound,
    There was a fair maid dwelling,
Whom I had chosen to be my own,
    And her name it was Barbara Allen.

2 All in the merry month of May,
    When green leaves they was springing,
This young man on his death-bed lay,
    For the love of Barbara Allen.

3 He sent his man unto her then,
    To the town where she was dwelling:
'You must come to my master dear,
    If your name be Barbara Allen.

4 'For death is printed in his face,
    And sorrow 's in him dwelling,
And you must come to my master dear,
    If your name be Barbara Allen.'

5 'If death be printed in his face,
    And sorrow 's in him dwelling,
Then little better shall he be
    For bonny Barbara Allen.'

6   So slowly, slowly she got up,
      And so slowly she came to him,
    And all she said when she came there,
      Young man, I think you are a dying.

7   He turnd his face unto her then:
      'If you be Barbara Allen,
    My dear,' said he, 'come pitty me,
      As on my death-bed I am lying.'

8   'If on your death-bed you be lying,
      What is that to Barbara Allen?
    I cannot keep you from your death;
      So farewell,' said Barbara Allen.

9   He turnd his face unto the wall,
      And death came creeping to him:
    'Then adieu, adieu, and adieu to all,
      And adieu to Barbara Allen!'

10 And as she was walking on a day,
      She heard the bell a ringing,
    And it did seem to ring to her
      'Unworthy Barbara Allen.'

11 She turnd herself round about,
      And she spy'd the corps a coming:
    'Lay down, lay down the corps of clay,
      That I may look upon him.'

12 And all the while she looked on,
      So loudly she lay laughing,
    While all her friends cry'd out amain,
      'Unworthy Barbara Allen!'

13 When he was dead, and laid in grave,
      Then death came creeping to she:
    'O mother, mother, make my bed,
      For his death hath quite undone me.

14 'A hard-hearted creature that I was,
      To slight one that lovd me so dearly;
    I wish I had been more kinder to him,
      The time of his life when he was near me.'

15 So this maid she then did dye,
      And desired to be buried by him,
   And repented her self before she dy'd,
      That ever she did deny him.

The Bailiff's Daughter of Islington

1 There was a youth, and a well belovd youth,
      And he was a esquire's son,
   He loved the bayliff's daughter dear,
      That lived in Islington.

2 She was coy, and she would not believe
      That he did love her so,
   No, nor at any time she would
      Any countenance to him show.

3 But when his friends did understand
      His fond and foolish mind,
   They sent him up to fair London,
      An apprentice for to bind.

4 And when he had been seven long years,
      And his love he had not seen,
   'Many a tear have I shed for her sake
      When she little thought of me.'

5 All the maids of Islington
      Went forth to sport and play;
   All but the bayliff's daughter dear;
      She secretly stole away.

6 She put off her gown of gray,
      And put on her puggish attire;
   She 's up to fair London gone,
      Her true-love to require.

7 As she went along the road,
      The weather being hot and dry,
   There was she aware of her true-love,
      At length came riding by.

8   She stept to him, as red as any rose,
        And took him by the bridle-ring:
     'I pray you, kind sir, give me one penny,
        To ease my weary limb.'

9   'I prithee, sweetheart, canst thou tell me
        Where that thou wast born?'
     'At Islington, kind sir,' said she,
        'Where I have had many a scorn.'

10   'I prithee, sweetheart, canst thou tell me
        Whether thou dost know
     The bailiff's daughter of Islington?'
        'She 's dead, sir, long ago.'

11   'Then will I sell my goodly steed,
        My saddle and my bow;
     I will into some far countrey,
        Where no man doth me know.'

12   'O stay, O stay, thou goodly youth!
        She 's alive, she is not dead;
     Here she standeth by thy side,
        And is ready to be thy bride.'

13   'O farewel grief, and welcome joy,
        Ten thousand times and more!
     For now I have seen my own true-love,
        That I thought I should have seen no more.'

The Great Silkie of Sule Skerry

1   An eartly nourris sits and sings,
        And aye she sings, Ba, lily wean!
     Little ken I my bairnis father,
        Far less the land that he staps in.

2   Then ane arose at her bed-fit,
        An a grumly guest I 'm sure was he:
     'Here am I, thy bairnis father,
        Although that I be not comelie.

3 'I am a man, upo the lan,
      An I am a silkie in the sea;
   And when I 'm far and far frae lan,
      My dwelling is in Sule Skerrie.'

4 'It was na weel,' quo the maiden fair,
      'It was na weel, indeed,' quo she,
   'That the Great Silkie of Sule Skerrie
      Suld hae come and aught a bairn to me.'

5 Now he has taen a purse of goud,
      And he has pat it upo her knee,
   Sayin, Gie to me my little young son,
      An tak thee up thy nourris-fee.

6 An it sall come to pass on a simmer's day,
      When the sin shines het on evera stane,
   That I will tak my little young son,
      An teach him for to swim the faem.

7 An thu sall marry a proud gunner,
      An a proud gunner I 'm sure he 'll be,
   An the very first schot that ere he schoots,
      He 'll schoot baith my young son and me.

Johnie Armstrong

1 There dwelt a man in faire Westmerland,
      Ionnë Armestrong men did him call,
   He had nither lands nor rents coming in,
      Yet he kept eight score men in his hall.

2 He had horse and harness for them all,
      Goodly steeds were all milke-white;
   O the golden bands an about their necks,
      And their weapons, they were all alike.

3 Newes then was brought unto the king
      That there was sicke a won as hee,
   That livëd lyke a bold out-law,
      And robbëd all the north country.

4 The king he writt an a letter then,
   A letter which was large and long;
   He signëd it with his owne hand,
   And he promised to doe him no wrong.

5 When this letter came Ionnë untill,
   His heart it was as blythe as birds on the tree:
   'Never was I sent for before any king,
   My father, my grandfather, nor none but mee.

6 'And if wee goe the king before,
   I would we went most orderly;
   Every man of you shall have his scarlet cloak,
   Laced with silver laces three.

7 'Every won of you shall have his velvett coat,
   Laced with sillver lace so white;
   O the golden bands an about your necks,
   Black hatts, white feathers, all alyke.'

8 By the morrow morninge at ten of the clock,
   Towards Edenburough gon was hee,
   And with him all his eight score men;
   Good lord, it was a goodly sight for to see!

9 When Ionnë came befower the king,
   He fell downe on his knee;
   'O pardon, my soveraine leige,' he said,
   'O pardon my eight score men and mee!'

10 'Thou shalt have no pardon, thou traytor strong,
   For thy eight score men nor thee;
   For to-morrow morning by ten of the clock,
   Both thou and them shall hang on the gallow-tree.'

11 But Ionnë looke'd over his left shoulder,
   Good Lord, what a grevious look looked hee!
   Saying, Asking grace of a graceles face —
   Why there is none for you nor me.

12 But Ionnë had a bright sword by his side,
   And it was made of the mettle so free,
   That had not the king stept his foot aside,
   He had smitten his head from his faire boddë.

13 Saying, Fight on, my merry men all,
    And see that none of you be taine;
For rather then men shall say we were hange'd,
    Let them report how we were slaine.

14 Then, God wott, faire Eddenburrough rose,
    And so besett poore Ionnë rounde,
That fowerscore and tenn of Ionnës best men
    Lay gasping all upon the ground.

15 Then like a mad man Ionnë laide about,
    And like a mad man then fought hee,
Untill a falce Scot came Ionnë behinde,
    And runn him through the faire boddee.

16 Saying, Fight on, my merry men all,
    And see that none of you be taine;
For I will stand by and bleed but awhile,
    And then will I come and fight againe.

17 Newes then was brought to young Ionnë Armestrong,
    As he stood by his nurses knee,
Who vowed if ere he live'd for to be a man,
    O the treacherous Scots revengd hee 'd be.

Mary Hamilton

1 Word 's gane to the kitchen,
    And word 's gane to the ha,
That Marie Hamilton gangs wi bairn
    To the hichest Stewart of a'.

2 He 's courted her in the kitchen,
    He 's courted her in the ha,
He 's courted her in the laigh cellar,
    And that was warst of a'.

3 She 's tyed it in her apron
    And she 's thrown it in the sea;
Says, Sink ye, swim ye, bonny wee babe!
    You 'l neer get mair o me.

4 Down then cam the auld queen,
        Goud tassels tying her hair:
    'O Marie, where 's the bonny wee babe
        That I heard greet sae sair?'

5 'There was never a babe intill my room,
        As little designs to be;
    It was but a touch o my sair side,
        Come oer my fair bodie.'

6 'O Marie, put on your robes o black,
        Or else your robes o brown,
    For ye maun gang wi me the night,
        To see fair Edinbro town.'

7 'I winna put on my robes o black,
        Nor yet my robes o brown;
    But I 'll put on my robes o white,
        To shine through Edinbro town.'

8 When she gaed up the Cannogate,
        She laughd loud laughters three;
    But whan she cam down the Cannogate
        The tear blinded her ee.

9 When she gaed up the Parliament stair,
        The heel cam aff her shee;
    And lang or she cam down again
        She was condemnd to dee.

10 When she cam down the Cannogate,
        The Cannogate sae free,
    Many a ladie lookd oer her window,
        Weeping for this ladie.

11 'Ye need nae weep for me,' she says,
        'Ye need nae weep for me;
    For had I not slain mine own sweet babe,
        This death I wadna dee.

12 'Bring me a bottle of wine,' she says,
        'The best that eer ye hae,
    That I may drink to my weil-wishers,
        And they may drink to me.

13 'Here 's a health to the jolly sailors,
    That sail upon the main;
  Let them never let on to my father and mother
    But what I 'm coming hame.

14 'Here 's a health to the jolly sailors,
    That sail upon the sea;
  Let them never let on to my father and mother
    That I cam here to dee.

15 'Oh little did my mother think,
    The day she cradled me,
  What lands I was to travel through,
    What death I was to dee.

16 'Oh little did my father think,
    The day he held up me,
  What lands I was to travel through,
    What death I was to dee.

17 'Last night I washd the queen's feet,
    And gently laid her down;
  And a' the thanks I 've gotten the nicht
    To be hangd in Edinbro town!

18 'Last nicht there was four Maries,
    The nicht there 'l be but three;
  There was Marie Seton, and Marie Beton,
    And Marie Carmichael, and me.'

The Bonny Earl of Murray

1 Ye Highlands, and ye Lawlands,
    Oh where have you been?
  They have slain the Earl of Murray,
    And they layd him on the green.

2 'Now wae be to thee, Huntly!
    And wherefore did you sae?
  I bade you bring him wi you,
    But forbade you him to slay.'

3 He was a braw gallant,
     And he rid at the ring;
   And the bonny Earl of Murray,
     Oh he might have been a king!

4 He was a braw gallant,
     And he playd at the ba;
   And the bonny Earl of Murray
     Was the flower amang them a'.

5 He was a braw gallant,
     And he playd at the glove;
   And the bonny Earl of Murray,
     Oh he was the Queen's love!

6 Oh lang will his lady
     Look oer the castle Down,
   Eer she see the Earl of Murray
     Come sounding thro the town!
   Eer she, etc.

Hughie Grame

1 Gude Lord Scroop 's to the huntin gane;
     He 's ridden oer monie a moss an muir,
   An he has grippit Hughie the Græme,
     For stealin o the bishop's mare.

2 An they hae grippit Hughie the Græme,
     An brought him up thro Carlisle town;
   The lasses an lads they stood by the wa's,
     Cryin, Hughie the Græme, thou 's no gae down!

3 They ha chosen a jury o men,
     The best that were i Coventry,
   An fifteen o them out a' at anse,
     'Hughie the Græme, thou art guiltie.'

4 Than up bespak him gude Lord Hume,
     As he sat at the judge's knee;
   'Twentie white ousen, my gude lord,
     If ye 'll grant Hughie the Græme to me.'

5 'O no, no, no, my gude Lord Hume,
    For sooth an so it mauna be;
For war there but twae Græms o the name,
    They sould be hangit a' for me.'

6 'T was up than spak her gude Lady Hume,
    As she sat by the judge's knee;
'A peck o white pennies, my gude lord,
    If ye 'll grant Hughie the Greame to me.'

7 'O no, O no, my gude Lady Hume,
    For sooth an so it sal na be;
For war there but twae Greames of the name,
    They soud be hangit a' for me.'

8 'If I be guilty,' said Hughie the Græme,
    'Of me my friends sal hae nae lack;'
An he has luppen fifteen feet an three,
    An his hands they war tyed ahint his back.

9 He 's lookit oer his left shouther,
    To see what he coud see,
An there he saw his auld father commin,
    An he was weepin bitterlie.

10 'O had yer tongue, my father,' he says,
    'An see that ye dinna weep for me,
For they may ravish me o my life,
    But they canna banish me thrae the heavens hie.

11 'Fare ye weel, Maggie, my wife;
    The last time I came oer the muir,
It was you berievt me o my life,
    An wi the bishop playd the whore.'

The Gypsy Laddie

1 The gypsies came to our good lord's gate,
    And wow but they sang sweetly!
They sang sae sweet and sae very compleat
    That down came the fair lady.

2 And she came tripping down the stair,
　　And a' her maids before her;
As soon as they saw her well-far'd face,
　　They coost the glamer oer her.

3 'Gae tak frae me this gay mantile,
　　And bring to me a plaidie;
For if kith and kin and a' had sworn,
　　I 'll follow the gypsie laddie.

4 'Yestreen I lay in a well-made bed,
　　And my good lord beside me;
This night I 'll ly in a tenant's barn,
　　Whatever shall betide me.'

5 'Come to your bed,' says Johny Faa,
　　'Oh come to your bed, my deary;
For I vow and I swear, by the hilt of my sword,
　　That your lord shall nae mair come near ye.'

6 'I 'll go to bed to my Johny Faa,
　　I 'll go to bed to my deary;
For I vow and I swear, by what past yestreen,
　　That my lord shall nae mair come near me.

7 'I 'll mak a hap to my Johnny Faa,
　　And I 'll mak a hap to my deary;
And he 's get a' the coat gaes round,
　　And my lord shall nae mair come near me.'

8 And when our lord came hame at een,
　　And speir'd for his fair lady,
The tane she cry'd, and the other reply'd,
　　'She 's away with the gypsie laddie.'

9 'Gae saddle to me the black, black steed,
　　Gae saddle and make him ready;
Before that I either eat or sleep,
　　I 'll gae seek my fair lady.'

10 And we were fifteen well-made men,
　　Altho we were nae bonny;
And we were a' put down for ane,
　　A fair young wanton lady.

Get Up and Bar the Door

1 It fell about the Martinmas time,
    And a gay time it was then,
When our goodwife got puddings to make,
    And she 's boild them in the pan.

2 The wind sae cauld blew south and north,
    And blew into the floor;
Quoth our goodman to our goodwife,
    'Gae out and bar the door.'

3 'My hand is in my hussyfskap,
    Goodman, as ye may see;
An it shoud nae be barrd this hundred year,
    It 's no be barrd for me.'

4 They made a paction tween them twa,
    They made it firm and sure,
That the first word whaeer shoud speak,
    Shoud rise and bar the door.

5 Then by there came two gentlemen,
    At twelve o clock at night,
And they could neither see house nor hall,
    Nor coal nor candle-light.

6 'Now whether is this a rich man's house,
    Or whether is it a poor?'
But neer a word wad ane o them speak,
    For barring of the door.

7 And first they ate the white puddings,
    And then they ate the black;
Tho muckle thought the goodwife to hersel,
    Yet neer a word she spake.

8 Then said the one unto the other,
    'Here, man, tak ye my knife;
Do ye tak aff the auld man's beard,
    And I 'll kiss the goodwife.'

9 'But there 's nae water in the house,
    And what shall we do than?'

'What ails ye at the pudding-broo,
   That boils into the pan?'

10 O up then started our goodman,
    An angry man was he:
   'Will ye kiss my wife before my een,
    And scad me wi pudding-bree?'

11 Then up and started our goodwife,
    Gied three skips on the floor:
   'Goodman, you 've spoken the foremost word,
    Get up and bar the door.'

The Farmer's Curst Wife

1 There was an old farmer in Sussex did dwell,
    (*Chorus of whistlers*)
  There was an old farmer in Sussex did dwell,
  And he had a bad wife, as many knew well.
    (*Chorus of whistlers*)

2 Then Satan came to the old man at the plough:
  'One of your family I must have now.

3 'It is not your eldest son that I crave,
  But it is your old wife, and she I will have.'

4 'O welcome, good Satan, with all my heart!
  I hope you and she will never more part.'

5 Now Satan has got the old wife on his back,
  And he lugged her along, like a pedlar's pack.

6 He trudged away till they came to his hall-gate;
  Says he, Here, take in an old Sussex chap's mate.

7 O then she did kick the young imps about;
  Says one to the other, Let 's try turn her out.

8 She spied thirteen imps all dancing in chains,
  She up with her pattens and beat out their brains.

9 She knocked the old Satan against the wall:
  'Let 's turn her out, or she 'll murder us all.'

10 Now he 's bundled her up on his back amain,
   And to her old husband he took her again.

11 'I have been a tormentor the whole of my life,
   But I neer was tormented so as with your wife.'

The Sweet Trinity

1 Sir Walter Rawleigh has built a ship,
       In the Neather-lands
   Sir Walter Rawleigh has built a ship,
       In the Neather-lands
   And it is called The Sweet Trinity,
   And was taken by the false gallaly.
       Sailing in the Low-lands

2 'Is there never a seaman bold
       In the Neather-lands
   Is there never a seaman bold
       In the Neather-lands
   That will go take this false gallaly,
   And to redeem The Sweet Trinity?'
       Sailing, etc.

3 Then spoke the little ship-boy;
       In the Neather-lands
   Then spoke the little ship-boy;
       In the Neather-lands
   'Master, master, what will you give me
   And I will take this false gallaly,
   And release The Sweet Trinity?'
       Sailing, etc.

4 'I 'll give thee gold, and I 'le give thee fee,
       In the Neather-lands
   I 'll give thee gold and I 'le give thee fee,
       In the Neather-lands
   And my eldest daughter thy wife shall be.'
       Sailing, etc.

5 He set his breast, and away he did swim,
   Until he came to the false gallaly.

6 He had an augor fit for the nonce,
  The which will bore fifteen good holes at once.

7 Some ware at cards, and some at dice,
  Until the salt water flashd in their eyes.

8 Some cut their hats, and some cut their caps,
  For to stop the salt-water gaps.

9 He set his breast, and away did swim,
  Until he came to his own ship again.

10 'I have done the work I promised to do,
  For I have sunk the false gallaly,
  And released The Sweet Trinity.

11 'You promised me gold, and you promised me fee,
  Your eldest daughter my wife she must be.'

12 'You shall have gold, and you shall have fee,
  But my eldest daughter your wife shall never be.'
       For sailing, etc.

13 'Then fare you well, you cozening lord,
  Seeing you are not so good as your word.'
       For sailing, etc.

14 And thus I shall conclude my song,
      Of the sailing in the Low-lands
  Wishing all happiness to all seamen both old and young.
      In their sailing in the Low-lands

Glossary

a': all, every
aboone: above
ae: one
aff: off
afore: before
ahint: behind
ails ye at, what: what's wrong with
ain: own
alld: old
almos: almost
amain: with force; at once
amang: among
an: and; if; one
ane: one
ance, anse: once
aught: owed (aught a bairn to: had a child by)
auld, aull: old
awa: away
ay: ever

ba: ball
baed: abode, waited for
bairn: child
bait: halt, give a rest to
baith: both
ban: bound, tied
bat: but
bed-fit: foot of a bed
beir: bear
bespak him: spoke up
bide: await, undergo
biggin: building
birk: birch
blaw, blawn: blow, blown

blude, bluid: blood
blue: blew
boddë: body
bonny: attractive, fair, fine
borrow: set free
bot: but
boun: bound
bound: indentured
brae: hillside
braid: broad
brand: sword
brast: burst
braw: fine, handsome
bree: broth
brigg: bridge
broo: broth
brotch: broach
but: except
burn: brook
byre: cowshed

ca: call
carlin(e): old (woman)
castin: cast, throw
cauld: cold
channerin: fretting
chap: knock
cheik: cheek
closs: enclosure, yard
cod: could
coost: cast, throw
cork-heild: cork-heeled
corps: corpse
couldna: couldn't
craw: crow
cum: come

49

dag-durk: dagger
dang: struck, thrust
daw: dawn
dee: die; do
deight: fitted out, adorned
deid: deed
deir: dear
didna: didn't
dine: dinner
dinna: don't
dois: does
doole: grief
dore: door
drap: drip
drie: suffer, undergo
dule: grief

eartly: earthly, human
Edenburough: Edinburgh
ee, een: eye, eyes
eight: eighth
eldern: old
eneugh: enough
erst: before, earlier
even: smooth
evera: every

fa: fall
fadir: father
faem: foam
fain: gladly
fairlie: wonder
fan: when
far: where
fash: trouble
fatt: what
feir: fear
feit: feet
fitt: foot
flang: flung
forbye: off to the side
forlorn: lost

fra, frae: from
frie: free
fun: furze

gae: go
gallaly: galley
ga'n: going
gane: gone
gang: go, walk
gar: make, cause to
gear: goods
gie: give
gin: if
gine: contrivance; given
girds: hoops
glamer: charm, spell
gleed: glowing coal
goud, gould, gowd: gold
gouden, gowden: golden
gowan: daisy
greet, grat: weep, wept
grew: Greek (?) (hound)
grippit: gripped, seized
grumly: fierce-looking
gryte: great
gude, guid: good

ha: hall
had: hold, keep
hadna: hadn't
hae: have
haf: half
hame: home
han: hand
hap: hop
hathorn: hawthorn
hauke: hawk
hersel: herself
het: hot
hichest: highest
hie: high
hir: her

huggell: hug, huddle
hussyfskap: housewifery
hyest: highest

ilka: every
intill, into: in
Ise: I'll

jimp: slender

kame, keame, kem, kemb, kemm:
   comb
ken: know
kirk-yard: churchyard
kitchy-boy: kitchen boy
kye: cows

laigh: low
lailly: loathsome
laith: unwilling
lake: pit
lan: land
lane, your: alone, by yourself
lang: long
lap: leapt
lasten: last
late: let
lauch: laugh
Lawlands: Lowlands
lea, lee: lie (tell untruths)
least: smallest
leman: lover
leven: glade
liften: lift
lig: lie (recline)
lillie, lilly, lily: lovely
lit: alighted
loe: love
luppen: leaped
lye: lie

machrel: mackerel

mack, mak: make
mailison: curse
mair, mare: more
make: mate
mantile: mantle
mary: maid of honor
maun: must
mauna: mustn't
meatt: food
meikle: much, great
men: mend
mettle: metal
mider, mither: mother
middle: waist
mirk: darkness
mirry: merry (standing phrase
   for followers)
mist: missed
monie: many
morne, the: tomorrow
muckle: much
muir: moor
mysel(l): myself

na, nae: no, not
nane: not at all
neer: never
nere: near(er)
nextin: next
nicht: night (the nicht: tonight)
nie: nigh, near
nourris: nurse

o: of
oer, owre: over
or, owre: before, ere
ousen: oxen

paction: agreement, compact
pall: fine cloth
pat: put
plaidie: cloak

prime: very early in the day
pu: pull
puggish: thieving, tramplike (?)

quin: queen
quo: said

rade: rode
reid: red
require: ask for
richt: right
rid: rode
rive: tear

sae: so
sair: very, sore, hard
sall: shall
san, *sane*: since
sang: song
sat: salt
scad: scald
schip: ship
schoone: shoes
schoot, *schot*: shoot, shot
scoup: move hastily
se: sea; see
sen: send
shathmont: six inches
shee: shoes
sheugh: furrow
shill: shrill
shoone: shoes
shouther: shoulder
sic, *sicke*: such
silkie: seal
siller: silver
simmer: summer
sin: sun
slack: gap, pass, morass
sma: small
sooth, *for*: in truth
soud, *sould*: should

spak: spoke
speir: ask
spiek: speak
stane: stone
stap: stop, abide
steid: steed
stran: strand, beach, shore
strang: strong
stroake: stroke
sud: should
suit: sweet
sum: some
syke: trench
syne: then

tacke, *tak*: take, took
taen, *taine*: taken
tane, *the*: one of them
teir: tear
tell: up to
tett: lock (of mane)
thame: them
thegither: together
thimber: heavy, massive
thrae: through
thresel-cock: thrush
thou 's: thou wilt, you will
thu: thou, you
tine: lose
tinny: tiny
tul: till
twain: two
twin'd: separated
tynë: tiny

unshemly: unseemly
upo: upon

wad: would
wadna: wouldn't
wae: woe

Wallace wight: a hero like Sir William Wallace
wan: wand
war: were
wardle: world (wardles make: earthly mate)
warsle: wrestle
warst: worst
wax: grow, become
we: with
wean: child
weel: well
weet: wet
well-fared: good-looking
wha: who
whaeer: whoever
whar: where

whatten: what
wi: with
wife: woman
win: wind
winna: won't
woe worth you: may woe come to you
wood: crazy
worm: serpent
wot: know
wrang: wrong
wul: will

yallow: yellow
yeir: year
ye's: you will
yestreen: last night

Alphabetical List of Titles

Alphabetical List of First Lines

DOVER · THRIFT · EDITIONS

All books complete and unabridged. All 5³⁄₁₆″ × 8¼″, paperbound.
Just $1.00–$2.00 in U.S.A.

A selection of the more than 100 titles in the series:

FLATLAND: A ROMANCE OF MANY DIMENSIONS, Edwin A. Abbott. 96pp. 27263-X $1.00

DOVER BEACH AND OTHER POEMS, Matthew Arnold. 112pp. 28037-3 $1.00

CIVIL WAR STORIES, Ambrose Bierce. 128pp. 28038-1 $1.00

THE DEVIL'S DICTIONARY, Ambrose Bierce. 144pp. 27542-6 $1.00

SONGS OF INNOCENCE AND SONGS OF EXPERIENCE, William Blake. 64pp. 27051-3 $1.00

SONNETS FROM THE PORTUGUESE AND OTHER POEMS, Elizabeth Barrett Browning. 64pp. 27052-1 $1.00

MY LAST DUCHESS AND OTHER POEMS, Robert Browning. 128pp. 27783-6 $1.00

SELECTED POEMS, George Gordon, Lord Byron. 112pp. 27784-4 $1.00

ALICE'S ADVENTURES IN WONDERLAND, Lewis Carroll. 96pp. 27543-4 $1.00

O PIONEERS!, Willa Cather. 128pp. 27785-2 $1.00

THE CHERRY ORCHARD, Anton Chekhov. 64pp. 26682-6 $1.00

THE AWAKENING, Kate Chopin. 128pp. 27786-0 $1.00

THE RIME OF THE ANCIENT MARINER AND OTHER POEMS, Samuel Taylor Coleridge. 80pp. 27266-4 $1.00

HEART OF DARKNESS, Joseph Conrad. 80pp. 26464-5 $1.00

THE RED BADGE OF COURAGE, Stephen Crane. 112pp. 26465-3 $1.00

A CHRISTMAS CAROL, Charles Dickens. 80pp. 26865-9 $1.00

THE CRICKET ON THE HEARTH AND OTHER CHRISTMAS STORIES, Charles Dickens. 128pp. 28039-X $1.00

SELECTED POEMS, Emily Dickinson. 64pp. 26466-1 $1.00

SELECTED POEMS, John Donne. 96pp. 27788-7 $1.00

NOTES FROM THE UNDERGROUND, Fyodor Dostoyevsky. 96pp. 27053-X $1.00

SIX GREAT SHERLOCK HOLMES STORIES, Sir Arthur Conan Doyle. 112pp. 27055-6 $1.00

THE SOULS OF BLACK FOLK, W. E. B. Du Bois. 176pp. 28041-1 $2.00

MEDEA, Euripides. 64pp. 27548-5 $1.00

A BOY'S WILL AND NORTH OF BOSTON, Robert Frost. 112pp. (Available in U.S. only) 26866-7 $1.00

WHERE ANGELS FEAR TO TREAD, E. M. Forster. 128pp. (Available in U.S. only) 27791-7 $1.00

FAUST, PART ONE, Johann Wolfgang von Goethe. 192pp. 28046-2 $2.00

THE SCARLET LETTER, Nathaniel Hawthorne. 192pp. 28048-9 $2.00

A DOLL'S HOUSE, Henrik Ibsen. 80pp. 27062-9 $1.00

THE TURN OF THE SCREW, Henry James. 96pp. 26684-2 $1.00

VOLPONE, Ben Jonson. 112pp. 28049-7 $1.00

DUBLINERS, James Joyce. 160pp. 26870-5 $1.00

A PORTRAIT OF THE ARTIST AS A YOUNG MAN, James Joyce. 192pp. 28050-0 $2.00

LYRIC POEMS, John Keats. 80pp. 26871-3 $1.00

THE BOOK OF PSALMS, King James Bible. 144pp. 27541-8 $1.00